The Tattooed Desert

Winner of the United States Award
of the International Poetry Forum

1970

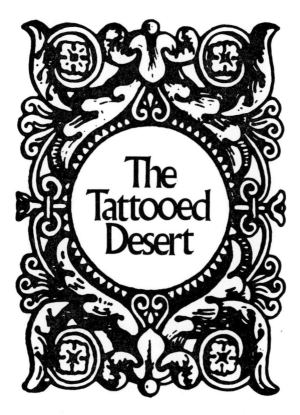

The
Tattooed
Desert

RICHARD SHELTON

UNIVERSITY OF PITTSBURGH PRESS

Library of Congress Catalog Card Number 76–134489
ISBN 0–8229–3212–1 (cloth)
ISBN 0–8229–5219–x (paper)
Copyright © 1971, Richard Shelton
All rights reserved
Henry M. Snyder & Co., London
Manufactured in the United States of America

Grateful acknowledgment is made to the following publications in which some of these poems first appeared: *Chicago Tribune Magazine, Inscape, Kayak, Lillabulero*, the *Outsider*, and Barent Gjelsness's *Changes*.

"Report of the Unsatisfied Lover" from "Six Reports from the Age of Mirrors," "Rendezvous," "Saturday Night at the Elk's Club," "October," and "The White Hotel" were first published in *Poetry*.

"New Year's Eve," "He Who Remains," "Valediction," "Reunion," "The Tattooed Desert," and "Connais-Tu le Pays?" first appeared in *The New Yorker*, © 1970 The New Yorker Magazine, Inc.

Contents

III The Scars

IV The Crossing

V The Tattooed Desert

THE
FORGETTING

for Lois

Gambit

I have boarded up the stations of waiting
where mice buy tickets to nowhere
and windows listen for announcements
of broken glass. Let the hands
of dead clocks rest
on the final numbers of chance.
The distance is over.

I have discarded the menu for lunch
and the menu for dinner. Each day
I choose something different to forget
and clear light arrives, bringing
the sea as it should be, the boats
where they are. I go forward
while irreplaceable leaves drip
from green cages and spiders
are playing their webs like guitars.

In one hand I carry your picture
to guide me and with the other
I am combing your name through my hair.

My Woman

my love with the alternate spelling
has never been gone and already
she is arriving from a place she carries with her
walking down the ramp as if she owned it
the hostess of scars

with her companion the coal
she has come a long way
see the stretch marks on her belly
the tears tattooed on her cheeks
I can repeat her from memory

naked among the chinoiserie
with her breasts in her hands
she comes to meet me
and pleasure runs like cool water
from her dilated eyes

she is the oracle in a grove of lilies and salt
having known it all before
and forgotten nothing

September

This is for the Piper and the Piper's
son if he has a son.
I will pay them both
someday
when I can no longer remember spring.

But tonight I wade
through fingerprints the trees
have discarded, dragging a shadow
of my almost ruined body
over September's dry waves.

Minutes have been grabbed from me
one by one and hours
slide into the ocean like seals.
When I look straight up
the stars
seem to be falling sideways.

Must I go back
to the same door and ask it again
am I worthy
and get the same equivocation?

There are so many others
but the night says this one,
a dark nest with its secrets waiting.

When I arrive I should say to you
lover
you are no longer young. Do not
depend on your beauty in the darkness.

But I will say nothing.
I can think only of the smell of rain
on my hands
after I have touched you.

Today

walked in the front
door and out the back, going
somewhere important,
while the mountains still waited
to be fed and the water
made thousands of sudden decisions.

Now the moon reaches
under the curtain with its tongue.
Wild camels run
through the desert. This is
the floor of the sea
many years later, the breakdown
of organized contemplation.

In a different empire
petty kings would be inspecting
ranks of thumbs at attention
and slaves would be chanting
for miracles in leather,
but we cannot afford mice. Even
spiders visit us rarely
and hurry away to more
comfortable quarters.

I see now that we have
made a success of our failures
and when tomorrow arrives
I will set the dogs on it.

October

The mountains are slowly dying
from lack of light while you and I
search for our twins through a dark
empire of anomalies. I am like the frost,
reluctant to touch you.
A ragged cottonwood rocks in its own arms
and fragments of rebuilt days
fall into vortices of shale and amber.

We are strangers. This is
the last dismay of the season.

Where do words go when they get tired
of being spoken and October's cold tongue
approaches the grove of deciduous nipples?

Letter from an Inland Province

late in the afternoon
when the light walks up and leans against me
I stand there like nobody I ever heard of
I just stand there

the poets have gone in search of words
and the prophets stayed home to wait
but I am a depot to which the trains
stopped coming years ago

once I saw long rubbery arms
torn up from the sea like snakes
I heard what the sand was saying
I listened all night while a monacle
chattered to the moon on the water
it was madness a kind of magnificence

I still know the words but I forget to pray them
it has never been easy
fighting the desire to eat glass

Men as Trees

I am something washed up on the shore
not knowing where I came from
or to which continent I belong

always I arrive at the same place
but lately I have been getting there sooner

carrying silence
hidden somewhere within me
waiting to be heard
and the answer for which there is no question
shifting it from one hand to the other
holding it out to strangers who turn away

each time I ask for more time
and get a smaller portion

in this place the desert comes right down
to the edge of the water
there is no margin for truth or error

no one is given a choice
of what he will love or be afraid of
yet we pay what we have
if we do not have enough
we pay what we have anyway

each a canary in his own cage
with his own mirror
and each sings to the bird in his mirror

and the sea runs up on the shore
throwing its hair back from its face
rolling before it shells half eaten by sand
while all the trees in the desert
walk through the night in search of love

New Year's Eve

The year is boarding
a clipper ship with frozen sails.
Soon it will depart through the terrible
refraction of water, carrying
dust in its mouth.

It had nothing particular
to recommend it, no Halley's comet, no
quintuplets, no two-headed calf.
It leaves no watermark on the wallpaper.
Yet it was sweet, it was sweet to us.

It was built from the raw
materials of small disasters and a summer
when the birds ate all the peaches.
We feel as if we have been telling
stories to which no one listened.

And it leaves behind a display case
from which each of us chooses his own dead
hands. The hands fit us
like gloves and we slip them on.
We stand on the dock
clutching our dead gods and old
poets while it lingers like the afterbirth
of sound, the silent bombast
at the terminal of memory.

The Source

I no longer worry about god let him
worry about himself
I have gotten over that

but years ago when you were
happy and smiling at the windows
I noticed they were getting dark

through one broken pane I saw
a map on which the names
of dead rivers
were crossing each other like stars

in our forbidden world I had begun
to despair
I tore myself in half
and said *this is my friend*

so they put me in a slimy room
with no one but an old sorrow
who crawled around on the floor
looking everywhere for his lost knife

there must have been
lieutenants behinds the scenes
cleaning up after me bringing me
food and being very careful
never to let me see them

my words collided in the doorway
none would go first
not one
I had nothing to give but my screams
and who wanted them

then one day I sat down
near myself and said *well well well*
took a deep breath
and forgot everything

you must save something
for tomorrow they told me but I was
laughing and shouting with happiness
it is all gone

now I find out what I am doing
by doing it
this is how I survive and if suddenly
I touch your face it is a new face
do not try to remember

April

returns like an expatriate, a defector
from the frost. Her feet are wrapped
in old rose petals, her eyes
are the color of wet sand under moss.

She guides a wounded caravan
of spiders and dilapidated memories.
Combing her dripping hair with elegant
fingers, she announces the forsythia and pain.

She waits in the summerhouse
for summer while the moon comes in empty,
a ship bearing her transparent name.

Under the Bridge

two cripples
prepare to make love
in a nervous canoe

their crutches
nestle like legs
against one another

several of the most important
events of the century
go by unnoticed

the river is getting
ready has been
getting ready for a long time

we offer prayers
to the god of delicate
processes and cast
our jewelled graffiti
on the water

The White Hotel

when winter comes
adjust your voice to it when the clock
dies hide it from the children

do not resist the urge to travel
it will be only a journey
and there is no arrival

drive through the desert
quickly it is inhabited by those
in search of death
you have as many minutes
as the rain has eyes

beside a gabardine sea you will find
the white hotel where bougainvillea
drips from the roof like blood

dim lights will be on in the hallway
a long moss carpet
flowing past a wilderness of doors
stairs crowded with unpredictable
lovers and assassins

in the bar new arrivals
celebrate reunions by throwing
their glasses into the fireplace
others just drop them on the floor

when anything falls down
in this hotel it lies there forever

all night they will sing
old songs *when the shoe tree
blooms in the desert and the ice plant
melts by the sea* all night
the water will rest
quietly in its blue tomb

at dawn when palm trees
wave their arms as they do at the slightest
change in plans you will watch
the waves send up
fine contingents of water

each retreating without losing its courage
thousands of white truces
negotiated on the sand

and with your pulse beating for distance
your hair turning to salt
you will say *because of its great
depth the sea can forgive anything*

but do not linger
at the white hotel or soon you will learn
that memory is the only
kind of loss we ever know

for John Weston

THE
COMMUNION of
STRANGERS

History

always on the horizon someone
is holding up a red thing
like a butchered cow its eyes
are as distant as old photographs

we invent the past we give it
to anyone who happens along it is
a bottomless lake with only
one shore and near it
we build our contradictions
towers with both clocks and bells
steps leading up to a blind wall

I do not understand war or history

the signs read *this way out*
it is a long way and there were
so many people I loved so many
people I could have loved

Eden After Dark

today
must have been Sunday
all the flowers were closed

the river which brought us
news of the battle
has been chained to its bed

even under torture
the map refuses to name names

the words we saved
for an emergency are gone
leaving us
with the terrible irony of gestures
which should have been made

in a paradise of burned bridges
the sadness is everywhere
we are already tired
of the war and there is
so much killing left to be done

we have given up sleep

at night we close our eyes quickly
and fall forward
into the arms of despair

Rendezvous

All day I have been
one transparent hand
praying to the other
avoiding the insolence
of empty elevators.

Now it is evening
and a sparrow searches through
popcorn and dog manure
trying to make this
one last trip worthwhile.

Tree! Tree! The wind
has left you forever.
You lean against dry air
like the ghost of yourself.
You are up to your knees
in the earth and dying
faster than birds realize.

It must be some kind
of salvation. With my veins
aching for the knife I arrive
at the communion of strangers.

Saturday Night at the Elk's Club

Entering, I find friends everywhere.
Those who can afford to be gracious
lift their glasses to those who cannot
afford to pay for the drinks. We
are all brothers here. We tell
prophetic lies and wait.

A girl comes in. She is nobody's
daughter. She is like a virgin
wearing petals of the flowering peach.
When she lies down it is
for a purpose and when she rises
it is for her pay. She says
For love this time, only for love.
Nobody believes her.

The door is locked. Someone
gets up to make a speech.
He says *For love this time, only
for love.* Several of us have our guns
ready but I shoot him. They hold
me down and pound my face
until morning arrives dragging Sunday
behind it like a tired slave.
We are all brothers here.

Six Reports from the Age of Mirrors

1. *Report of the Driver*
Sooner or later the calendar
goes down on her back
in every man's bed. I was
born on the way to the hospital
and died on the way to the hospital,
strapped on a table, counting
backward from ten to one. With
my name checked off the list,
my number memorized, my number
forgotten, it was a fast ride
down a chute of bells and sirens.
The thermometer froze in my mouth.

2. *Report of the Missing Child*
It was a game. I crawled
into the abandoned icebox.
Now leather and dust compare
memories of me while roots
pry through the floor.

3. *Report of the Drunk*
Water under the bridge, water
over the dam. I accept this life,
I reject this life, I drink
too much, I die drinking,
I am resurrected on a dry morning
past my prime, did I have one?
I fall into the river
and am washed up several miles
downstream in the middle
of a picnic carrying
rosemary, saffron, and wolfsbane.

4. *Report of the Black Widow*

I listen for the web's
vibrations and repeat by rote
what I cannot bear to remember.
Jumping up when my name
is called, accepting my mission,
I will carry your luggage of skin.

5. *Report of the Pilot*

It was simply that the parachute
failed to open. Having
lost my irredeemable accent,
I held my memories down
with a tongue depressor and quickly
consulted a map of the world.

6. *Report of the Unsatisfied Lover*

Morning approaches our naked
bodies. The good shepherd,
insomnia, leads his sheep
over a cliff and pain walks
through the land of erotica.
The age of mirrors on the ceiling
is over, my darling,
and some of us missed it entirely.

The Mute

The stones are given out
one to a customer. I keep mine
separate. With such a companion
why should I want anyone else?
And we know how to get home,
it is downhill all the way.

I stand with the same string
over my shoulder, holding out
the same bowl. Streets
stretch out from me like patience.
People pass by with their other
lives, looking away. I want
to give them the bowl,
but I am ashamed it is empty.

The thing I lost between the lies
and the prophets, and could never
find again, was it only
my velvet tongue? Even
the mountains have questions to ask
somebody, but they are afraid.

So I continue to tell my story.
Each time I start at a different
point. If I walked backward
into the past no one would miss me,
but I could not find my word
there. My word is not
bread, as some imagine.
It is in another language
and I am a man of little learning.

The river has scars which it
never speaks about. My secrets
are safe with the river. I could
give it my address if I had one.
It would not rob me. It moves by
in dignity, without trumpets,
proud of its bridges. It knows
the combinations of wheat fields
far away. It knows this is
the wrong place, that the light
here is all reflected. It knows
that every night is part
of this night. It says *trust me,
be silent, I will read the cards.*

When the rain comes I retire
behind a curtain of needles and look
at the world through their eyes.
I would not have wanted the birds
with their tiny pointed tongues
to go thirsty another night.

Notes from the Night Watcher

tonight I have crossed bridges
of insomnia and found the moon
playing its tiny piano

ships pass me in the desert
they are in a hurry they will not
stop for anybody

the road hops away on one leg
it needs to lean
on someone's shoulder

night and morning are making
promises to each other
which neither will be able to keep

after the battle is over
I will find the body of darkness
between two hills
fallen in a good cause
and who is to say it was hopeless

Autobiography

1

birds on the pump handle
cattle dying of thirst
memories in windows

dawn as it
begins to bleed
the blood mixes with water

it hides behind mountains
pushing the mountains in front of it
put your ear to the ground and listen

I have the keys
in my pocket but I will not
go back there

2

with my tongue on her hand
my hand on her breast

I said to her
death I said

I am waiting for something to happen
is it my move or yours

pick up an old shoe she said
and learn from it

there was always a reason
she said but I have forgotten

He Who Remains

you have so much to give they said
so I gave it now it is gone

I stand with my back to a cliff
where stones lean over
looking down at me they are smooth
they have dragged themselves
a long way to get here

years ago I wrote love letters
to distant water and wore
the desire to travel like a hair shirt

but that is over and regret
was never a friend of mine so I
let him go in search of the others

who departed wearing accidental lives
mocking me calling me *he who remains*

and I remain in the desert
caught in the ropes of myself like
rosaries staying here with penitent
stars whose confessions frighten me

there is no explanation for lights
which move about inside the mountains
and coyotes are all that is left
of a race we once conquered

at night I hear them worshipping
gods with unspeakable names

I have learned to make use of pain
he never fails to take me
into his confidence telling me
more than I wanted to know

and when morning arrives bringing
whatever it can to help I ready myself
for the impetuous revival of sand

if I were to leave this desert
who would cherish transparent
light who would nurse broken stones
who would mother the cold

The Past

mask I have worn and discarded
staring with blind eyes at the mountains
how does it feel to be there
when the light arrives to meet you

The Way Back

begins here
in the eyes of a stranger
and moves past tomorrow without speaking

past the girl in the long black dress
to the girl in no dress at all
going with the raga
down between her breasts

the way back leads along an avenue
where hands are growing into their gestures like trees
and I carry the mystery of darkness
safe in my pockets

past the sound of clapping hands
where deaf children
sit on the fence like birds
past widows' hands
which are frames holding their broken windows
past turquoise hands opening and closing like doors

I find my own hands discarded
one holding the other

I see the needs of the sycamore
denied
and hear the cottonwoods telling the truth
with no one to believe them

the way back turns on itself
turns
and is silent
entering a geneology of mountains
each its own monument

the bridges
wave to the river and the river says only good-by

I find my footprints and follow them
backward
into a a grain of sand
where the light in its old age
has few visitors
and its brother has no proper name

the way back bypasses special days
whose owners
stand guard at their doors
it circles the brooch with a missing stone
it leads past the bullet waiting in its chamber
like sperm in a testicle
past the wounded target eager to die

past the embryo
timing itself for birth

the way back
leads to a point in the future
where all I have ever been
will arrive and I will say
without flinching
yes
it is mine

Strangers

we find ourselves at the exact place
where the light becomes darkness
and turn our faces toward one another

realizing we could be lovers we could
be anything we could even be friends
we could carry our scars
like banners we could pray to each other
and answer each other's prayers

this is the earth we can touch it
the mountains expose their nipples
to the last rays of the sun
and day lingers on the undersides of leaves

with so much need on the horizon
surely there is a heart around here somewhere
but we are characters from a book who have
come here on vacation
to listen to the pulse of the sea
which makes an affirmation beyond despair

those who have heard it
do not recommend it to anybody

we have heard the hypnotized telephone
ring itself into a trance of silence we have
seen the poor pass by on borrowed legs
we have been enameled by the sun

and as we are slowly going under water
where all light
is the light of a green stone broken open
we keep our distance it is all we have

THE
SCARS

Leonard Shelton
August 7, 1901—November 1, 1969
. . . nobody rich or famous . . .

Reunion

once a year at midnight
the ghost of my father walks
in wearing his scars
on the outside of his bandages
asking directions *which
way are we going
how far to silence*

maps flapping on the walls
the walls falling in and me
waiting as usual while the future
limps from door to door
on its broken toes

sliding into a chair
and tucking one leg under him
his bloated head begins
to fall toward his right
shoulder as he gives me a long

wink and says *I'm going
to get drunk again tonight
god how I dread it*

Scene of the Accident

a spot marked on the map with a white cross
just off the road
where the desert ceased
and farms had hardly begun

I would not have called it
a destination
or even a good place to spend the night

but I recognized everything

a few scars left over from earlier battles
one spoon with its eye half-closed
in a dry ditch with a sign
here slept and your name and the date

suddenly my immaturity got up
and bounced away
sending off sparks
like a chain dragging behind a truck

while I chased after it
calling all your lost names

August

All summer
surrounded by unconditioned air
my father has been dying.

Anybody coming by here
at night
could see me looking out the open window
and wonder what I am waiting for:

the stars to move perhaps,
the big dipper on its delicate
hinges to tilt,
the earth to cool.

Today smelled like burning rope
and tonight the moon is cut in half.
Promises are unimportant to us now.
The past is sufficient.

I choose his memories with care
and hold them
before vague eyes
as if they were charms on a string.

Life drops
from his white hand,
a scarab falling into thick grass,
and the look on the face of silence
is surprise.

Surgery

you watched them at work
with their knives and scissors

you watched them sewing you up
hope with his needle and thread
attacking the helpless eyes of your buttons

knowing that all you really needed of yourself
was the part they would not let you keep

November

1

when I arrived
stone crosses hung from the eves
and ambulances were lined up at the door
like hungry mice

the wound I left here years ago
I asked them
has it healed yet

your father is sleeping they told me
come back tomorrow we are
closed for the night

but just at that moment
out of breath and wearing
somebody else's clothes
a funeral rushed into the hospital
barely in time to rescue the dead

2

before that I was saying
something different I was
a flag trying to escape from its pole

now I enumerate the qualities of silence
first the stars which are pores
in the skin of night then my birth
which did not include me
then each leaf falling
as one wing flying away
without its mate

3

my father went in search of death
like a mole
blind and beautiful

all summer he listened
to the inner voice of his pain
rising in a song clear and high
dragging the music after it

his life was an unmade bed
nobody rich or famous ever slept there

he put his face into the fire
and said *I will not keep you waiting*

4

wherever the rain goes tonight
I will go with it
through the city I was born in
city of monuments the statues their
lethargy their cold wet faces

the names of the streets
are climbing into the mountains
and the mountains are holding their names
up to a dark sky

weeping birches continue to weep
for us and for each other
I cannot comfort them

I carry myself in my own arms
past the houses of the important where
they live among their habits
as comfortably as water on stone
the doors are asleep
in the arms of their hinges
I leave them sleeping

at every step
darkness seeps from the holes in my shoes
I am cold as an empty glove

from the sidewalk
I pick up a black walnut
locked in its shriveled skin like a mummy
father I say to it tenderly
old father it was harder than hell
to love you
and impossible not to

look what november has done to us both

Cortege

inside a lung somewhere
a star is falling

the widow
is what is left over
she will get used to it

in the meantime
the mourners have been paid
and dismissed they can
go home we can
all go home

where the tongue
we left on the windowsill
to ripen in silence
is beginning to wake up
and speak
the exact words of the dead

Instructions for Finding Water

From your bundle of scars
take one which has
the shape of a forked tongue
and hold it level in front of you.

Start walking in any direction.
Vega, the falling vulture,
will guide your steps
straight into the desert.

Do not be afraid when the wind
rings you like a leper's bell.
Only the man who has nothing
to leave behind him
can divide his possessions
equally among his children.

December

The trees are a blond haze
scarred by empty nests of magpies.
The road follows me at a distance
and I come back to this place
with nothing in my hands for the river,
telling the gospel of winter,
every word true
and no one to believe me:
the snow is dying for all of us.

I come back like an empty
revolver, hoping that something
will happen here to change
the past, but the same gray board
is nailed to the same tree
and the past remains. I pile up
a small mound of stones
for its monument. This is where
the words died and I
buried them. Now I am wearing
my tongue for a coat.

The Search

Because the journey would no longer
wait, I took it. I put fresh
bandages on the photographs and set
the silences in their proper places.

Then I went out to meet you, ghost
at the corner of my eye dressed
in the rags of your curious profession.
I was trembling like a fork struck
in a wall when I got to the graveyard
where we had shared so many
bottles of cheap pain, where the dead
grew in such profusion and you knew
everybody. But you were not there.

So I followed the clock who was
full of religious motives,
lurching toward his heart attack
on the coast of inquiry. And while
the sponges were dying of air
and pink starfish left their last
messages in the sand I watched you
drift off with the tide, followed
by a retinue of luminous sharks.

I called you back but you
had already forgotten your name
and did not answer. Now when Saturday
arrives still in Friday night's
clothes and workmen climb
their scaffolds to put up the sky
I hear only the voice of the sea
but I listen anyway. It is my voice.

I stand on an unfinished beach
where nobody ever comes and hear
myself shouting *rescue, rescue.*

Questioning the Dead

the keys I carry
suggest a need for locks
but there are no locks and you
who lived here before
could help me if you would

can I believe
what the rain says about you
your postures your stiff agility

is truth the girl
whose father beats her in secret
who hangs her head over the river
and stares at the reflection
of her bruised face

must I make up my own song
every winter
and sing it to frostbitten ears

do you believe me
you could know better than I
where I have been
and what I have forgotten

I went to the place of hands
and found them empty
except for one closed fist
holding my name

Not Many Years Later

when the end in view
is no longer visible and the string breaks
each pearl will set off
in search of its own oyster

the banished
will return falling like yellow dust
over their native stones

I will find my brother and sister
silent as stones
waiting in the middle of the road
and farther on
my mother
whom I never discovered
and my father who never discovered me

my wives
waiting to be loved my children
waiting to be born
and me with my shoes
so perfectly alike
in the corner

my motives will count up their losses
and go home
where I will arrive like a burn
carrying its scar
and find truth
familiar spirit
smelling of the sweat
of bodies I had forgotten
hanging from a nail
in the wall of an old house
miles away

Prayer to the God of Darkness

I travel by night
through the phases of a lost moon
and you move beside me always
like the horizon

you are the stone I carried
on my tongue through the desert

when I give gifts
you have no hands when I
sing songs you have no ears

let the darkness
honor its promises

I hold out my hands to you
you rest on my shoulder

let my talk be the rhetoric of scars

when I tell your story
no names will ever be mentioned

THE
CROSSING

for Brad

The Voices

Suddenly dawn
had to get up and build the trees.

I could no longer deny
the voices so I came
to terms with them: glistening
votaries dipped in madness,
a blue eye in the wrong socket,
an old chair
rocking by itself,
leather with its memory and silk
which forgets everything,
a machine producing time
in the factory.

This does not mean
I learned to trust them
but I came to terms with them

because, as they said,
we are the only family you have.

Near Water

I find myself again
after a long absence.

The lake becomes another color.
It listens. The crows
are arguing fiercely. They all settle
into the branches of one tree
and pull darkness in after them.

Surely I do not live here
where the water has no pockets
and nothing to carry.

I would go with the music
if it would take me. I would even
go with silence if I knew its name.

But where did I come from to get here?
Which train did I catch?
Who waved good-by?

The Children

I heard the mouths of the silent
dying of departure

if we could only remember
the water before it froze
they said

learn this I told them
it is not true
but it will keep you warm in winter

my words
fell on their delicate shoulders
like whips

we are thirsty they said
their dry laughter was desperate

take this cup I told them
and wait for the rain

put your wilted hands
over your eyes
and believe in the coming of light

The Coat of Many Colors

The message always reaches me.
It comes over the speaking tube,
the grapevine, in the yellow words
of sand about to be shifted,
in the sweet alphabet of the diabetic.

The carpenter has fallen off the roof.
Come back at once to the King
Queen and Jack you were dealt.
Wrap your coins in tissue paper
and return to the family of water.

And I return like a discarded theory
still remotely possible. Each
time it is later. It is the same
but the stones we hold are smoother.
We have been talking to somebody
else and we have forgotten.

This time we know where the coal lives
and what it complains of. We have
discovered how many grains of wheat
to leave on a grave for birds.
When we find old aunts and uncles
hidden under the stairs, we bring them
out into the light and they crumble.

Those of us who lie have become
better at it. Those who try to tell
the truth are spies without passwords,
smuggling bits of silence
past the sentries and photographing
the contents of empty safes.

One reaches into his pocket
and finds a fish. Another returns
the yellow eye she borrowed years ago.
Our talk is the communion of upper
and lower dentures. Our words
are an exact distance from one another.

At night we watch the artificial
flowers closing. We have dreams
about dreams we had before.

Each tells his story. The oldest
sat in a web and waited for the spider.
The youngest stayed home to raise
the flag on the mailbox. One watched
the fishbowl go dry. One gave up
hope at midnight and ran with Cinderella
down a dark road to the river.
One found out what the necrophiliac
does after he opens the coffin.

The night gets cold. Our fire goes out.
The furniture is too ugly to burn.
They give me a coat of many colors
and I put it on. We join hands
for the seance. There is one hand
left over. It touches my face
as if it were the hand of a new lover.
It traces bloodstains on my coat.

Who are you, Spirit? they ask me.
Where do you come from? When I answer
my voice is disguised with distance.

I am the map you drew of an unknown
desert land. It was more
accurate than you imagined. In that land
we expose our memories to the weather
and they die. We live without them.

See what the sand has done to my eyes
and let me return to my country.

The End of the Line

we have traveled all night
through a kingdom of telephone poles
where smoke loses
its virginity and pale whores
promenade around graveyards
with the dignity
of animals followed by fire

through cities of albino bricks
behind which lovers hold each other
in beds of venetian glass
and on past empty
boardinghouse porches where
those who are married to chairs
have taken them inside for the night

intravenous light comes through
the moon a transparent chip
cut too thin to be of any use
and we arrive at the distant
point of departure
glad to be back
as if we knew all the time
we were traveling in a circle

this is where everybody
gets off the bus and walks
away in a different direction
even the driver

a small town where the clock
on the abandoned courthouse
runs backward but who needs
it whoever needs it

at the edge of town
I find a large house
the last of its kind with its
lights still on in derision

the furniture is authentic
mother-of-pearl the chandeliers
are old aunts hung up with sachets
in their pockets
the banisters are polished ice
melting into the carpet

all faces here are reflected
on water and crustaceans
of eyelids have formed on their eyes

from the mantels small stone birds
look down with questioning faces

in the garden the dew is searching
everywhere for the body of the nonmurdered
while inside they move
from room to room
lifting masks on photographs

this is the house where
suicides meet to celebrate
their artificial family ties

I will keep it in mind

for Steve Orlen

The Crossing

The journey is always return.
What I cannot leave behind I take
with me: my hands like dry vines
torn from a wall, the memory
of strangers, the smell of wet sidewalks
worn into the soles of my shoes.

Just after dawn the river exposes
its wound and I cross a bridge
in love with its own reflection.
A few lights are still on in houses
downriver. A rowboat half sunk
in the mud is calling for help.
Even from this distance I can tell
the trees are crippled with age.

I am full of other places and tired
like birds who return in the spring.
I stumble through jonquils the color
of flesh, past holy places
where lovers and children have made
nests in the matted grass.

They are flying flags in the city
of flags, so many at half mast,
so many in my honor. They keep up
appearances. I enter the city
through a gate as old as smoke
and have returned to my own people.

Those beside whom this river
passes always, will they forgive me
the distance? Those without eyes
who count days by fingering notches
on sticks, those who grow thin
in silence, who do not permit
their clothes to touch their bodies,
who have only their names to guide them.

I walk among them. They bow
two by two, with their arms
around one another. The signs
say *Keep Moving*, the flowers are stone
faces covered with moss. I had
no idea the dead lived so well.

Connais-Tu le Pays?

I have discovered a country
where the pages of books are all
margins and the calendar is frozen
in a wall of ice. Its mirrors are kept
in cages and covered at night.

I cross its border by way
of the labyrinth in the radiator.
The doors close behind me.

The guards at the gate of the principal
city are dangerous. Also
the porter who hangs on the wall
like a silver knife. As for the troll
who once lured me under a bridge,
I blame him for everything.

There is no map of the city
but I know my way.
When I get to my room
the others are waiting: the child
with tiny blue fish in her hair,
the ghost with a flashlight,
the prince who died of a bloody
nose and the angel who guards him,
the white nun dragging
her long black shadow.

I show them the sand I have
smuggled in my shoes, and my letters
written on dry grass.
I bring them a yellow wax
flower in a green pot.
We celebrate the silence.

At night when it rains we paint
a small fire on the wall
and sit before it, drinking
from cups made of buttons.
We drink to the present which is
eternal. We drink to the delicate
shells which grow in the garden,
to salt rising up
from the earth like smoke,
to another safe journey.

Outside, the water is moving
past in search of some
low place to lie down.

The Unexpected

translucent ribs open
like venetian blinds it is
autumn I recognize the distant
skyline I am in the suburbs
of my city the abyss

saying *brothers brothers*
holding out my hands
as keys to a double lock
hail detritus keeper of gates

my footsteps have fallen
like drunks on the pavement
let them sleep where they lie
there is a continuity in death
I had not expected

sympathy who would never stay
where I put her sneaks off
around the corner of a funeral
her smile is a nervous tic

purple widows approach
they have rinsed their hair
in nacre for my arrival they
welcome me to the charisma
of asters and rain

the stars still ask
irrelevant questions and I am
still no good in that direction
preferring to look at the wounded
uncomprehending trees they
blame no one

memory has gone who knows where
taking its futile gestures
now deserted places can speak
in their own voices
in the present tense

and I hear the rain which has
always required so little of me
saying *summer is over*
it is time to look about for a new
lover under the fallen leaves

Valediction

I who witnessed the nail's desire
for a blind hammer
and kept account books of rain

have got through the day without hope
what an accomplishment
now I can drop my eyes like stones
into the black water of night

I am taking myself apart
like a puzzle

this must be an ear this must be
a piece of my coat
or is it sky which there is so much of
and all the same color

I am resigning from my shoes
they are worn out
and will fit anybody

whoever wears them
his job will be to harvest
the wrinkled shells of walnuts

he must remember the signals
how to speak
to ducks about their carelessness
how to remind trees they have
a certain responsibility

he must prevent the sleepy road
from stumbling into the river
and watch for tiny fish
who swim past
carrying great burdens of light

THE
TATTOOED
DESERT

The Tattooed Desert

at whatever page the book fell open
I read it
and knelt beside every bed

they could have baptized me
in any tub and fitted me with second hand
wings at the auction
I wouldn't have minded

but the gods turned out to be
grotesques they paraded before me
as if for inspection with dirty gauze
over their eyes
when the road forked they took
both ways they disguised themselves
as places I couldn't find
their feathers turned into ferns and when I
reached out to them
they were distant landscapes
moving through my fingers and leaving
a strange smell on my hands

while the old hat under the tower was telling
the same story and a toothless mouth
was getting ready to grin
the one with a face like a pig
began to eat his own fingers
and I ran away

they initialed the space I left
empty but they found me again
upstairs in the back bedroom of another house
with whisky hitting my tongue
like a hammer
and again I climbed out the window and slid
down a tree in the gothic rain

I must have been almost crazy
to start out alone like that on my bicycle
pedaling into the tropics carrying
a medicine for which no one had found
the disease and hoping
I would make it in time

I passed through a paper village under glass
where the explorers first found
silence and taught it to speak
where old men were sitting in front
of their houses killing sand without mercy

brothers I shouted to them
tell me who moved the river
where can I find a good place to drown

slowly they raised their heads
this is the tattooed desert they told me
all that will survive of it will be
what you remember
then they went into their flaming
houses and closed the doors

and I rode on through the disappointed night
with my pulse beating like a ticket about
to be torn while the mountains tried
every possible position and finally
slept with their backs to one another

when I found the river it was
what I expected just an old wall lying down
covered with pictures

dead mystics were buried on its banks
each with his telephone beside him I recognized
the place I knew all the secret
passages it must have been
where I was born

the gentle eyes of the river
looked up without reproach and those
floating past spoke to me
this is cremation by water they said *we who are
burned here rise up without ashes
we are repeated
in the sound of wax bells ringing
and the testimony of mouthless trees*

while they spoke the sky arrived
and I saw the perfect complexion of light
the wind was blowing the mountains away
at an incredible speed and suddenly
it was the morning after nothing

my faithful servant Pain
who had followed me all this way
approached holding out a gift and I took it
a sleeping bat gorged with blood

all day I will carry it with me
as a reminder to those who try to take me back
see I will say
holding it up to them
we have survived another night

COLOPHON

The type used for the poems in this book is Lino-
type Palatino. It was designed by Hermann Zapf
and named in honor of the famous Italian scribe.
It is used here in the ten point size, leaded two
points. The cloth is Fictionette, by Columbia Mills,
and the paper is Warren's Olde Style. The book
was designed by Gary Gore, and printed direct-
ly from the type by Heritage Printers, Inc., of
Charlotte, North Carolina.